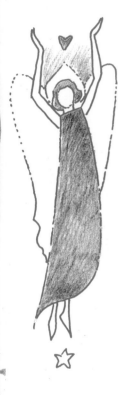

To: _____

From: _____

BelleTress Books, a division of Red Wheel/Weiser & Conari
Press with offices at 368 Congress Street, Boston, MA 02210

Published 1994. Second Edition 2003
Printed in China
10 09 08 07 06 05   8 7 6 5 4 3
Library of Congress Catalog Card Number 94-60742
ISBN: 0-9708754-8-7

www.redwheelweiser.com

100 WAYS TO ATTRACT ANGELS

by SAMARA ANJELAE

illustrated by ANCA HARITON

BelleTress Books

Dedication

To 100 souls from birth to present who have shared their wings of love, humor, kindness, creativity and wisdom.

Mom, Dad, Lew & Toni, Mike, Sis & Flip, Gye-Gye & HoHo, Granny Johnson & Bob, Jamie & Chip / Mrs. Pierce, Mrs. Elkins, Mrs. Davenport, Mrs. Traylor, Mrs. Stephens / Sammy Albright, Celia Finger, Harriet Hillard, Benji Rankin, Kelly Galbraith, Rosemary Stevens, Lucy Alverson, Ricky Mingua, Wayne Stocker, Jimmy Flippin, Ginny Brown, Lynn Bowers, Kay Garraway, Milton Robichaux, Janet Graves, Linda Underwood, Jerry Caffey, TU Black, Karen & Lane McDaniel, Laura Young, Jerry Johansen, Julie Rask, Allen Smith, Barb & Phil Laporte, Aimee Porter, Bonnie Brandel, Judy Jost, Cheryl Eastbourne, Jan Nygren, Echo & Mae Bodine, Jeff Bolin, Jessie & Matthew Bolin, Katy, Stina Dascola, Monica Hennessy, Carol Delong, Patsey Kahmann, Megan Alford, Rick Holloway, Tom Linzmeier, Paul Van den bossche, Maureen Griffin, Martha-Elizabeth Ferguson, Carolyn Jones, John Moore, George Sourati, Dan Kindeleher, John Haile, Julie Dungan, Brad, Hardy, Marilyn Dungan, Suzanne Rogers, Beula Fraley, Judy & Earl Behning, Anca Hariton / Rudolph, Little Gray Kitty, Simon, Shoo-Shoo, Stray with no name, Daisy, Willyshine, Bigfoot, Isabella, Lady Woot, Ellie, Tamara, Dante, Solo, George Elliot, Skyra / Celia, Samuel, Tabear, Gabriel, and Ashlea.

family / teachers / classmates, friends & co-workers / animals / angels

Introduction

You are ready, to be touched by an angel, to see an angel, to feel the presence of an angel, and to know an angel. I invite you to open your heart, go deeper than you have gone before. Dedicate a moment of your love and time to acknowledge the heavenly messengers. Answers come, bringing joy and comfort into your life.

Each of the *100 Ways to Attract Angels* may be used to start or enhance your day. Some you may choose to spend more time on than others. If a way works for you to feel, see, or know the presence of an angel, then share that way with someone else who could use some angel love. Wings of love surround you, rays of light engulf you, and tears of joy await you.

Samara Anjelae

You have been here before. You will
be here again, each time blessed with more
wisdom and love. In angel time there are no
beginnings and no endings. By starting at
this place you will naturally attract angels;
angels for life, angels for eternity.

$\mathcal{T}$ake an Angel Vow.

I pledge to use the help of angels in all of my life affairs and transactions, knowing that I don't have to travel this journey alone.

*Calm your mind, close your eyes.
Call the presence of your guardian angel.
Give your angel a name by openly
receiving and accepting whatever comes
gently into your thoughts. Maybe the
name will come one letter at a time, in a
vision, or through a sound. No matter how
your angel arrives it will be the appropriate
way for you.*

4

*T*ake a pencil and paper and write down a heart-felt prayer request. Ask that your requests be for the highest good of all. Now place the piece of paper in a sacred spot blessed with goodness, sincerity and love. Joyfully release your request to the care of the winged messengers.

5

Extend love toward all living creatures – from the tiniest of insects to the largest of animals. Make this a practice and you will have friends and joy throughout your life.

In a peaceful setting surrounded with beauty and stillness ask an angel to come into your life – gently, lovingly and gracefully. The moment you ask is the moment your request is answered. Angels are waiting for your invitation.

Turn your shadow into an Angel Reflection. Embrace all aspects of yourself – the people and animals in your life and everything in your world. Pick one thing, person, or situation that you normally complain about and try to look at it with love and without judgment. Soon you will recognize the angel in you and the angel in others.

Abide by the Angel Laws.

Always show your wings,
Radiate light even in darkness,
Make music wherever you go,and
Never leave home without your halo!

9

*S*oar high and far today. Imagine that you have your own angel wings. As you view your angel body, accept your presence with love and understanding. Go forth with strength and beauty, and spread your wings of light throughout the day.

Gently close your eyes for a moment. Draw your attention to the top of your head. Visualize a halo pouring white light down through your body. The light is filled with wisdom, love and truth. As you open your eyes say thank you to your angelic friend who brought you this gift of light.

Tell others of the angelic qualities that they possess. Let this be a reminder to always aspire to be an angel. When we are angelic in thought and action, then we naturally attract our heavenly companions.

12

*S*tand still and feel an angel touch
you with a gentle breeze and a light
touch. Let the soft energy of the angel's
wings embrace you. Now, give a hug to
the next friend you see. We gracefully
learn from angels.

Often angels speak to us through symbols. Their symbols help us remember who they are and why they visit us. When seeing their symbols acknowledge their meaning:

Halo, *symbol of innocence*
Trumpet, *the voice of God*
Lily flower, *symbol of purity*
Wings, *the delivery of Divine messages*

*D*edicate yourself to having your everyday thoughts and actions be a joyful prayer of gratitude to God. Angels serve and praise God. They invite your help. You may find an abundance of surprises coming to you.

15

Picture your favorite place. Now go to that place with the eyes of a child, seeing it like you have never really seen it before. Understand that angels are always with us. Sometimes we just have to adopt a new vision or a new attitude.

$\mathcal{A}$cknowledge an earth angel experience or be open to one. It comes when you least expect it and when you need it the most. The encounter might leave no trace except a feeling in your heart, a turn in a situation, or a moment of hope.

17

*M*ake something with your hands. Draw upon angelic light to guide the creative process. Creating with love brings passion, beauty and harmony to the heart, and joy to God. Be an artist today and create.

Visit a place of a nature, either mentally or physically. Feel wings of love surround you as you enter the beauty and solitude. Say words of appreciation as you reach out and speak to the trees, animals and birds. Feel the connection and become one with all.

Close your eyes and put your finger on one of these angel traits. Reflect on that quality and have your angel send it to you.

Abundance
Newness
Growth
Enthusiasm
Love

$\mathcal{B}$e a receiver today. A part of living is learning to receive as well as to give. Joyfully expect something good. Reflect on what you want to be brought to you, and release your wish to the winged messengers. Angels love to give to those ready to receive.

Travel the Angel Road where everyone is welcome. You will recognize the road where souls of all shapes, colors and cultures reside. Here there is a void of prejudices and judgements and a vacuum of acceptance and kindness. Make a decision today to accept and respect all who travel and reside on this road of life.

*B*egin a Spiritual Workout

Go on a walk and invite your angels,
Read an inspirational passage,
Volunteer your time, and
Surround yourself with lightness.

In silence angels talk. Set aside some time each day, even five minutes, to do an Angel Meditation. Ask that an angel touch your heart with a thought, word, whisper or feeling. Your world will be brighter as you receive an angel's love and light.

Angels resonate with sounds of love. Refrain from speaking negatively about yourself and others. Choose your words, thoughts, and actions carefully. Where there is love, angels reside.

*L*earn the universal language
of angels.

Speak with love
Touch with kindness
Listen with care and
See with beauty.

26

*W*hat you intend is what you
become. Intend to be the shining light
that you simply are. Start by seeking the
highest in love, light and truth.

In your heart know that you are–

Guided and Protected by Angels.

*W*here your attention goes, you go.
Focus on the virtues and strengths of
others as well as your own.
Empowerment comes from having
compassionate thoughts for all.

Plant an Angel Garden. Cultivate the positive traits of your personality, weeding out the unhealthy seeds. Gracefully make your inner life rich in harvest, bearing flowers and fruits. Perhaps visit a real garden for this Divine inspiration. Remember, gardens are the enchanted playgrounds of angels.

Within a day's time complete an Angel Mission. Do a good deed for someone(without telling anyone). Open your heart and heal a relationship. Send a positive thought to someone in need.

When you have completed the mission, listen for your angels to say thanks for a job well done.

Let go of an area in your life where
you are trying to be something you are
not. Surround this thought with light,
making it grow fainter and fainter till it is
completely out of sight. Angles love
originality, honesty and simplicity.

Be Yourself.

Create an Angel Treasure Map. On a piece of colored paper, place a picture of yourself and a picture that represents an angel. Then place symbols, words, and pictures that reflect your goals and dreams. Place the treasure map where you can see it every day. Then watch as you, God, and your angels manifest your aspirations.

*A*ngels thrive in happiness. Focus on a joyful experience. Recreate this special time by capturing the details and all the meaningful feelings. If you are unhappy, angels will patiently wait until you have changed your mood and outlook. In times of sorrow it helps to be reminded of a beautiful memory, especially of a loved one who has since moved on to spirit.

*B*ecome familiar with the Archangels
and their specialty.

Gabriel: Bringer of News
Raphael: Angel of Healing
Michael: Guardian of Peace
Uriel: Angel of Prophecy

*Call upon them as you need them, and
watch your creativity awaken, emotions
heal, harmony increase and ideas transform.*

*F*ind a place to do Angel Breath
Work. In a quiet place take a few deep
breaths. As you inhale, breathe in love
and light. As you exhale, breathe out
tension and fear. Keep taking deep
breaths until your mind, body and soul
are in harmony and at peace. When you
arrive at this state, you will have found
the place where angels reside.

Trust your feelings, even the painful ones. Listen to your intuition and the voice of your angels. Together they make a powerful combination. Know that you have answers within and joy is always in your reach even through sad and difficult times.

*S*ilently say,

I am loving, I am loved.
I am loving, I am loved.
I am loving, I am loved.

Angels are loving, and they love you.
Enjoy their company.

*R*epeat aloud to a friend or loved one,

You are loving, you are loved.
You are loving, you are loved.
You are loving, you are loved.

You have now spoken the language of angels. Very simply it is the language of love.

*D*evelop an Angel Habit. Call in a specific angel to help with a situation. For example, call on the Angel of Justice to help in a case of unfairness. Call on the Angel of Hope to surround you when you are feeling despair. Call on the Angel of Healing when you are in pain, emotionally or physically. Angels are waiting to serve.

Awaken your spiritual heart at the top of your breast bone. Softly place your hand there and tap the area. Each time you awaken your spiritual heart you awaken your senses to capture the essence of your angels. Create your own gesture or saying to draw your angels closer to you. It is especially helpful during your trying times.

Make an Angel Amend. Angels like to bring people together. Take the first move toward forgiving yourself and forgiving another. Forgiveness makes room for more happiness in your life.

41

*M*ake a lifelong commitment doing random acts of kindness. Be sure to include children, animals, the environment, and yourself in your generous good deeds. Angels will be there to inspire you along the way.

Listen to the sounds of nature. Clear your mind and become a channel for angels. Accept the messages that are brought forth. Pick up pen and paper and record your thoughts and words. Conversations with your angels may lead you on a journey to paradise.

43

Create an Angel Ritual: face north and call forth Archangel Michael, face south and call forth Archangel Gabriel, face east and call forth Archangel Uriel, and face west and call forth Archangel Raphael. You now have all your bases covered to participate in this game of life. Ask for their Divine guidance and protection.

*L*eave something better than how you found it and you will naturally attract an angel. Angels gladly assist in improving yourself, the environment, and the community. Whether others see you does not matter. Your angels see you.

Awaken to who you are. Accept the truth that you are now and always have been a Divine Being of all that God is – love, power, wisdom and life-energy. When you acknowledge your beauty, goodness and unique gifts, angels feel at home. They then feel welcome in your presence.

Reflect on a friend, pet, or loved one who has made transition to the other side, already in heaven. Send a prayer of love to that special one, knowing that at the appropriate time souls leave us and are reunited with us. Angels are transmitters of love and bridgers of realms.

47

Call for Angel Assistance and say a prayer. As you talk to God let your prayer be in your own words and from your heart. Be observant and open to the possibilities that will be presented to you. The heavenly messengers will respond with love and light.

*P*lace your hand gently over your heart. Listen and fell each beat. Softly with your finger trace the infinity symbol.

∞

As you trace this symbol fill it with angelic love. Know the love you send out will always return, tenfold.

49

*W*rite a letter to your guardian angel and celestial companions. Give thanks to them for being there even when you were unaware of their presence. Share your hopes and deepest thoughts. Know that you are always surrounded by heavenly messengers.

*S*mell your favorite fragrance,
perfume, flower or scented candle.
Surround yourself with fresh-cut flowers.
As you slowly inhale the fragrance, feel
the joy and bliss within you. Angels are
attracted to fragrant scents.

Enjoy an Angel Review. Reflect on your actions and events at the end of the day. Acknowledge where you could have been more angelic in your actions and words. Then acknowledge where you could have had angels assisting you.

*C*reate a spiritual space. Make it sacred with a beautiful cloth, candle and flowers. You may want to add special pictures, figurines, prayer beads, sea shells and so forth. Spend time in this space reflecting on your oneness with all souls. Enjoy and know your angelic companions will always feel welcomed.

_M_ake an Angel Wish List. In order
of priority make a list where you could use
an angel lift. Wait patiently for their
heavenly responses, giving gratitude as
your wishes come true.

Take a piece of paper and call forth your inner child. Joyfully and playfully draw the image of your guardian angel. Let your inner spirit guide you as you make contact with your angel visually, emotionally or physically. Angels will gladly assist you in your Divine work.

*S*tart an Angel Scrapbook for
yourself or for a young child. Begin by
collecting and recording acts of love and
goodness. Blessings multiply for those who
take the time to appreciate the many gifts
given to us.

*R*eflect on your name. Try to find the meaning and the feeling that goes with it. Now reflect on the word angel, messenger of God. Next, place the word angel before your name. Know that you too are a messenger. Spread some love and lightness with someone today.

Angel (your name)

Do an Angel Dance. Move in all
directions with grace, beauty and lightness.
Spin around in a clockwise direction
awakening each of your energy centers.
Flow gently with every move, making your
life the greatest dance of all. Invite an
angel to be your partner.

For this moment, do nothing. Just be. Enjoy some peace and quietness. Let the angels do the work while you give yourself a break. You will know when to move forward. When you are so busy, even angels have a hard time getting your attention.

*D*rop clues that you want your angel to appear. Believe and trust with an open heart, have sincerity in your request, discover your own inner light, and be ready to experience an abundance of angel blessings.

Be an Angel Communicator. *Communicate what you believe, and share your angelic experiences, not by force, but by love. Stand up for the rights of others. Children and animals especially need extra help. Angels will hear and applaud you.*

Create or purchase angel treasures –
books, angel statues, jewelry, cards,
pictures. *Angel reminders open the heart
and calm the mind to draw forth your
winged companions.*

*S*tart reading your Angel Horoscope *(it never changes),*

"You have free will to make today and every day how you want it. The power to create lies within you. Your guardian angel and your league of special angels are waiting to assist."

*S*end an Angel Beam. When someone near you is radiating negative or hurtful energy, beam them a beautiful stream of pink light. As the light engulfs them, bless them with peace and understanding. Send angel beams as often as needed. They work much better than unkind words or actions.

Call or write a family member or
friend who has been an angel in your life.
Says thanks in a warm and meaningful
way. Sometimes our dearest loved ones
do not know how we feel about them.
Take the opportunity to share your
thoughts while they still walk on earth.
This opens the passageway for more
angels to enter your life, seen and unseen.

*S*tart an Angel Journal, a keepsake of your dearest thoughts. Record your times of great joy, deep gratitude, special loves, unique animals and fortunate incidents. One may have many journals in life, as one may have many angels. Angels lend their wings of love to help create special moments to record.

Do a Wing Exercise. The next time you are having trouble getting someone's attention, visually and emotionally begin to fluff out your wings. Use your imagination and make your wings far and wide. Your angels will help you create a magical stir.

Be around babies and children and experience their innocence. Participate in their traits of laughter, gentleness and purity. Honor the child-like qualities in yourself and learn to take life a little more lightly.

Visually place pink and white light around you to instill calmness and healing. Move with peace, knowing an angel will appear when the heart and mind are ready. It takes only one word, feeling, or touch for you to experience the presence of an angel.

Clothe your body with a blanket of love. Think of words that describe your loving nature. While searching for the words, allow an angel to bring them to you. Know an angel brings only words of goodness and love.

Do a Releasing Activity. Take a thought that no longer serves your needs and then say,

"I completely release you to the care of my winged messengers."

Free yourself as you give thanks to your celestial companions.

*D*evelop and use your creativity.
With self-expression comes delight.
Attract an angel by expressing yourself in a
unique way today. Try your talent at
writing, speaking, singing, meditating,
maybe, even playing.

*T*ouch a friend with kindness.
Go out of your way to say,

"I love you."

Whether you choose to say it
silently or out loud, speak it with love
in your heart. Guardians of Truth will
carry the message long after the
thought and action.

*P*ut a smile in your heart and put a smile on your face. A smile says,

"*Love exists in my heart and I want to share it with you.*"

Now wait for wings of love to appear.

*W*hen you feel a little defeated, tired, or discouraged, clothe yourself in light blue to represent the celestial and heavenly spiritual energy, or clothe yourself in white, the pure light of illumination and wisdom.

*S*ay the word ANGEL.

A
*N*atural
*G*iver
*E*xpressing
*L*ove

Be ready to receive an abundance of love from the heavenly realm.

*A*sk for an Angel Message. Open a
spiritual book at random and reflect on
the passage where your eyes first fall.
You will be guided to the right page,
paragraph, or just the right word that
will tell you what you need to know.
Angels are guiding your hands. Use the
information wisely.

*D*onate or give something away. Whether the gift is of great value or little worth, something you love, or something you have outgrown, does not matter. What matters is, a loving gift that is given unconditionally to another will be returned, someplace in time. Angels complete the transaction.

Be aware of animal angels. Take the opportunity to communicate and connect with the spirit of an animal. Animals have much to teach us. When you give love and respect to animals, you are giving love and respect to God.

Give away Angel Gifts.

Compassion
Healing Hands
Open Attitude
Light Heartedness
Sense of Humor
Unconditional Love

*V*isit a wise soul. Here is your invitation to find an answer to an unresolved question. A wise soul could be a sage, teacher, healer, friend, or even your higher self. Wherever the journey takes you, angels will greet you at the visit.

Give nature a helping hand. Do not take from it but instead give something to the earth. As you offer your gift of love and respect, listen and feel the luminous beings of nature speak and embrace you with gratitude.

In order to fly with angels we need our feet on the ground. Become solid and stable by making an Angelic Arc between you and your angels.

*A*lign – be in the present
*R*eveal – a gift, talent, creative thought
*C*onnect – with your angels

Ignite your flame of joy and contribute to the happiness of another. Think of a simple good deed that you could do to make someone happy. Commune with your angels first, add your light, then spread your wings of love.

Do everything with love today. Make everything you do special and blessed with love, no matter how little it seems. The heavenly messengers feel at home where there is love.

Let go of judgements. Understand that the disapproving thoughts we have about others can often be projections of unloving thoughts we have about ourselves. When judgements leave, messengers of light enter.

Visually or physically make an Angel Hope Chest. Fill it with love, sincerity, wishes and dreams. Know it is you who holds the key to unlock the many treasures of heaven and earth. As you open the chest watch your angel:

Happily
Offer
Positive
Encouragement

*B*e extra kind to all living creatures.
Adopt, love, or care for a nearby animal.
Call upon the animal's angels to send
light, love and healing. Respect all of
God's creatures. Angels do.

*L*eave out angel treats – plants, flowers, fragrances, candles, beautiful cloths and inspiring music. Angels reside near all spiritual beauty.

89

*T*ake or start a spiritual class.
Surround yourself with other spiritual
seekers. Enjoy the company of like-minded
people as you journey into new learning.
The more we grow and expand our
knowledge, the more we see that there is a
universal angel-spark in all of us.

Angels gracefully aid in transformation. Choose a self-defeating habit you would like to eliminate. Take the first step by saying goodbye to it. Now write down one trait you want to adopt. Angels will support you in your desire, courage and progress.

Count backwards from ten to one. With each count say a blessing, such as having a supportive friend or having a healthy mind. When you arrive at number one, your heart will be enriched with enough angelic love to bring more blessings to you. Angels will deliver them with ease and grace.

*S*ay an Angel Affirmation.

*I am aware, accepting,
and receiving Divine
Angel Guidance in all
that I desire to know, to
do, and to experience.*

*V*oice an Angel Decree.

Reveal to me your true solution of this situation with which I seem to be most concerned. Come forth in thy perfect timing, wisdom and love.

Refine, but do not destroy, your human qualities. Think, speak and act with spiritual sensitivity. Make this a practice and you will find angels sensitive to you.

Look around and choose a symbol that represents the qualities of an angel – lightness, love, joy, peacefulness. The symbol might be a beautiful flower or your favorite bird. Now be open to anyone or any situation that might reveal this symbol throughout the day. It is your angel speaking to you!

*L*earn an Angel Motto.

Home is where you hang your halo.
Miracles are angels in motion.
Expect a miracle, receive an angel.

*H*onor what your mission is here on earth. An angel will aid you gently and lovingly, helping you carry your work in all your travels. When you are true to your path, angels rejoice.

*A*ngels love the sounds of beauty and truth. Write a poem expressing oneness, peace and love. After you have composed your piece, sing it your celestial friends and make them shine forth with delight.

*R*ight before you go to sleep ask for an angel dream, a dream to reveal what you most need to know at this time. Ask that you awaken with full remembrance, and with full understanding. Thank your angel in advance for sending the message.

By arriving at this place, you have naturally attracted angels; angels for life, angels for eternity. In angel time there are no beginnings and no endings. You have been here before and you will be here again, each time blessed with more wisdom and love.

Other books and journals
by Samara Anjelae

Angel Prayers
My Guardian Angel
My Fairy Godmother
My Magical Mermaid
Wonder Windows Gift Box
Fairy Journal: Thoughts & Dreams
Gnome Journal: Notes & Musings

www.belletressbooks.com